meanwhile

Celebrating
30 Years of Publishing
in India

'Beneath tide-pools, squid-spew and moon-slick water, these poems usher us into those places where nothing is as it seems. And yet, there is the pervasive magic of the everyday, where women in trainers may turn into antelopes, where sated cats know that fish are real things, and where a single glance at a tree can turn an entire world into "leaves". Prerna Gill's poems make their home in the gaps that can only be forded by image – between movie tickets and calcified stars, breakfast and meltwater, femur and sky. A restrained, assured and gently luminous collection.'

— ARUNDHATHI SUBRAMANIAM

'Images and emotions are woven beautifully – and sometimes startlingly – in these poems that rise from the depths of the heart.'

— CHITRA BANERJEE DIVAKARUNI

'This is a book of thoughtful poems about highly human figures framed against something else, something vaster: headlights, tarmac, sky, sea, distance, time. It is a collection to be read slowly and savoured.'

— TABISH KHAIR

'Gems both dark and bright, these are poems that will speak to everyone, because they balance the heart and mind between their lines. The effect is magical.'

– DHARMENDRA DEOL

'Prerna Gill's poetry is personal and honest. She is successful in reconciling her urban upbringing with her ancestral roots that require both vulnerability and courage.'

– SHABANA AZMI

'Prerna Gill's poems allow you to peer at conflicting emotions. Jagged outlines filled with lyrical beauty.'

– TWINKLE KHANNA

meanwhile

Poems

prerna gill

HarperCollins *Publishers* India

First published in India by HarperCollins *Publishers* 2023
4th Floor, Tower A, Building No 10, DLF Cyber City,
DLF Phase II, Gurugram, Haryana – 122002
www.harpercollins.co.in

2 4 6 8 10 9 7 5 3 1

P-ISBN: 978-93-5629-397-7
E-ISBN: 978-93-5629-398-4

Typeset in 11.5/17 Arno Pro at
Manipal Technologies Limited, Manipal

Printed and bound at
Thomson Press (India) Ltd

For

Vijayta Gill, Vivek Gill and Sahil Gill

Pulkit Deora and Anahat Gill-Deora

Contents

CONTENTS

Contents

CONTENTS

Author's Note

No, no, I recognize the shiny stuff too. Privileged childhood, check. Handful of 'first' loves, check. Growing my family and having the time to write – all of that too. With so much gratitude.

Seems a little narcissistic then, to put this book out – here to say that I have issues at all feels like undermining a lot of important voices around me. Perhaps all of them. So, I try to see this as an attempt to understand the less-than-shiny things that I can't quite ignore any longer. The everyday things. The things that let the shadows in.

I know most of my generation struggles with mental disquiet of some sort or the other. I won't list them. All I know is that some of us try to get away through all that books and movies and social media encourage us to celebrate. The 'wins' and 'big moments'. And all those fucking vacations – the most popular of band-aid solutions.

But what about when the guests leave, when the evening's last glass sits empty, when your partner is asleep and the room is far too still?

There seems to be no looking past the greys that string all the bits of colour. That's why I thought I might give in. Listen for once. Write. And here's what I have to show for it. Ramblings? Poetry? Symptoms? It's not for me to decide. Never was.

Visit

In the basement of my parents' house
Meet the rivers five
Quieter gods this lot
They discuss prices and poetry and squatters' rights

At first I hear them muffled
Glugging far beneath my bed
Until the pillow sends ripples
Across the sheets and crossed shadows
And I sink through deep green waters
To a cement floor buried
Under boxes, old chairs, a pantheon in a funk

And I cannot deny Hydaspes is the farthest
Bronze-thighed Jhelum has ever
Strayed from his silt for Sikander
And maybe battle glory

And I don't have the right verse to plead
Faiz and feminism to a lithe Chenab
And his retinue of ghosts unquiet:
Forever daughters to Waris Shah and the moon

Still it is difficult that Sutlej
Full-lipped Shatadru herself with that extra edge
From the darkest waters of Rakshastal
Will never speak beyond my pulse
Or explain why it is said

That even her witches spare
The seven homes closest to their own

An Hour Stays

I meant to look at the time
Just as the room stopped and
Left the clock to loom lunar over
Floorboards sinking under-tread
With every wood crevice running into veins
And pushing pulse to the beat of footfalls
From days to seasons ago

That is, before the room stopped, kept me
And kept me facing the door holding up a pillar
Of yellow hallway light
Its reflection slitting my eyes feline
Feral in a room caught in its shadows setting thick
And treacle-glistening
And pulling down these arms
Tar – it's always hungry in here

Unmasked

With oleander and toasted apples
Shirley Jackson hides cottagecore between ghosts
A light in the window to search by
Through lower shelves that fold
The spirit of final girls brave in gruesome tales
Who know only the pathos outside pathogen

Or maybe I'm just hard at not looking
At my neighbour reaching through the wall
Her name quaking my lungs
Setting the dust motes green
Glaucous moon shivering inches of glass
She cuts her shape, cuts at it in echo
Grows it asking after her sons and rent
The possibility of rain and grandchildren
And if they glimpsed her first body
In birthmark, headline, running stitch

Keeping

Childhood was small animals
Some mornings I think of a rabbit with orchid ears
The stray toms left her in a pit in my stomach
Filled with lettuce and sweet straw

For at least one yellow bird
It was more about the mess that remained:
Droppings greenly gumming feathers to bars
Around a seed-speckled spot of bright loss
Never named

Now I keep the cats in my home
And I move like a whisper
And I see in the dark

Cleaning

There is something
to be said about tradition
quiet as the pigeon feather
and smell of blue soap
clinging to the laundry line
making suds of smaller clouds

When we let moths out of Dadi's blanket trunk
does the sun work on the mites and little ghosts
that make words in the dust
leaving their echoes to bristle the lawn?

Does the sun work at us
like it does on the silverfish
removing flecks of doubt
folded between pages with
bodies dull and hard of vein
still clinging to words on yellow paper –
or are we just slow to fear in the spring?

Indiscretion

It should be simple:
Stand up
Wear your clothes
Leave

Framed taut by doorway he is patchwork:
One day sewn into another,
Unequal in their lamp-sepias and moon
Paisley and grain
Smoothing over furrow and clench
When I insist colours are proud things,
Assert I humble them well in my
Black-and-white that lets me sink into
Shadows resisting bedposts,
Framing, crossing pale cast of window:
Lilac box over rug and stain

So when he looks for me,
Turn the other way
As he closes,
Leave

Or Not Drowning

Come teatime she will inherit her ice

Until then this courtyard, this twig,
Hard peal yielding to prying
The bare moon-yellow flesh underneath
One of the season's best-kept secrets
Here for her fingers to come apart a little slower
Stealing her from sweat and rumbling thunder

And finally now
Her hair unravels
Upwards swaying dark as squid spew
As the cold marbles a sky beyond the glass surface
Forming now far above it quivers
Down the blue sunlight mottled by
Clumps of crystal now unfurling
A brinicle finger to touch her frozen
To the bed with the languid urchins, sea stars, blue worms
As all the fish school into the trenches
And the chalk and black coral graveyard sternly
Takes hold with all its grain
And still now

She reminds herself of girlhood
And documentaries
Of runaway underdog heroines
And of the deep-sea volcanoes
Keeping the glow-things with sulfur
With germ and with heat
Where she braces for the dark
Muscles crunching the frost until
She stops for the merfolk approaching
Flashing scales and paisley pasties and gilded cowrie
    cellphones:
The queen mother carrying the teapot, cups, kelp
Trailing, of course

Sister
Her smile

The Sand Children

At first frail
They crawl out of tide pools
Moon-slick water opening for:
Their bodies slow with mud-smoothed toes
Crescent ribs pushing sharp and
Eyes unblinking in salt air

Froth sweat and frantic hands
They reach back under the surface where
Black gathers between the rocks alive
With pincers and jelly and flaming stars

Grasping with a hunger for
Dreams folded in sea glass bright
In greens and blues of thunder

Sea treasures rolled hard
From broken bottles and mildewed words
They hold them tight as webbed fingers can

And send them small into their mouths
Gathering more in little fists
Like grapes and peaches and java plum

Until moments before a yawning sun
sees them melt to lavender foam
Away from city lights and windows where
Their sleeping, breathing lookalikes
will never dream again

Bhramari

Wings are not what she is known for
Smaller than a fingertip
They fan the marching summers
Into a hum before resting flat enough
To iridize green skies into winter sun
And back to June along their span
But all you remember is the sting – bright

Bright hot and sharp all and everything the world
Black and yellow

Wings are not what you know her for
They are language and if you listen close
You will learn my shadow is a swarm
And in the quiet: hive

Red

Said outside of medical books
And plain on every face in transit:
Some of us are grey by twenty-five years
At least the parts closed in our ribs

Red loses the deeper it goes
And here the kelp and pale coral
Here silence

Spring

It is to halve a plum on your plate
And stagger back in horror
At its syrup frothing wild

And blowing large its amber pit
Before it bursts to scatter
Melon, peach and apricots
Tumbling across the floor
To find you in a corner

On knees now rolling moss
Clutching at your swelling throat
As trembling hands pull from your mouth
Strings of gold laburnum
Bright in spittle-glitter

Until sweating ripe
With amaltas, you turn over
On a rigid back pushing tiles
Firm against all these vines
Snaking up your walls

And spreading there their nests
And thorns and treacle hive
Humming the stillness of your home
With this season's only warning:
It won't last long

Chedipe

Never told him enough
And so he remains
And so headlights through the window grills
Stripe his room sharp

With dusk and the disguise
In its sleeves and silks turning
To roadkill greenly on the floor

And his voice
In all its antler velvet
Roughs hers a growl when there
Is no lace between her
And her joints hitch and corner and split
Drawing paw-spans from sheet
To mirror and sink

Never could tell if she first saw him
From behind green bottles or tall grass

Caught

It was only a kite at first
Between branches for a day
For more

It was makeshift bright with wrapping paper
Silver pinning green stars
Thorny keen the way constellations prickle
The way the flesh is seized
Yes, portal to stark auroras
Nighttime and a paisa in a bowl

Shines sharper than its glassed string
Could halve a plain sky
Shines stern on my house now on this city
Now on the corduroy sea and its birthmark islands
Where we amble after names
Carry sugar cubes on our backs

The sun is silver if you miss winter at all
And today it is nearly right angled
And loved by a tree

No Strings

Blue from midnight windows
He asks in little

And here I listen
With pins in my mouth
Until agreed:

We will loosen our consonants
Drip lime to starburst between us
Until citrus pinwheels to sun
And we stripe with spun light
The quiet that lives between stars

Taken by hand pulled
Along for pinched gain
And sewn into half-past eleven
Through spans one shade of dark

We are gone and surfaced new
Zardozi with vertigo
So the sky could once be tapestry

Unspool now we are the colours
Of each other now until headlights and toast

Unspool

Everything Half Off

Even here, spare time begins to thicken
Cool and cornered in a changing-room mirror
I step out, no purchase, as the woman behind me births
Grunting into the heap of refused size Ms
Devouring a glossy placenta as the infant
Draws a bruised leash out to where the mall spreads
To neon, where even the neighing and
Breathless gossip from the food court
Cannot drown out the flies –

They know in our ribs and our warm bladders we are
Banquet and contender, queuing up at the till half-watchful
For wild dogs and discounts
On the latest fall fashions

The Dollmaker

She pulls undone
Her crisscross smile
And the thread falls with
The lace dress she sheds
Unbuttons her chest
To vent a ticking that
Counts to noon

She doesn't mind the mothball
And peppermint waft of
The room with red drapes
Stained glass high and
A clockwork door:
Its painted trees, clacking
Iron birds, trilling
Village folk, bobbing

The knob that plays
A melody as it turns
To announce the good doctor
With the kind button eyes

King

The Jackal loosened his tie
As though it were folk knowledge
As though he were ready to forget
That antler velvet and spidersilk
A throbbing wound would heal best
Now that it was out there in ink
Opinion, transgression, cry for the carrion:
Sedition to the top brass looking for the lion's share
And so he will have to lie low now
Or for now

The hotrod exhaust could play mist
To his lore, fable, alibi
His five o'clock shadow
Blue enough and
His fingers still smeared with indigo
Pretty much pinning him a still colour
In a street blinking invitations long past neon
As he lights up and slants into the alley

Meanwhile

With the swing of evening shadow
No he was here for the dead:
Clean up, spare thoughts, street-grade empathy

He cups the lighter closer now
Storm cloud crouching in clench of jaw
Letting go the nicotine plume:
A screen to make shadow puppets
Of uniforms closing in

Unseasonal

I know the farm folk ask
What time means to rain
Cupping a village in pigeon down
Where sun slants to comb
The sharpening rabi stalks

This is slick-wet under heel
This is sodden wood to fasten your door
I turn from pinpricks that remember salt
And when the sky is slowly plain
I find the storm hiding

In aparajita's quivering pout
Only she knows when it will return
To find the riverbanks parched

Dinner

Still at night I am in the hallway mirror
Approximations of sufficiency and want
Pressing close these resemblances to those
Who took longer to collect
From scraped knees to memories of deer
To very-tall tenants while
I hardly watch from here
Left to address and hum and eat
Roaming the meanwhile of curtain print
Unsmiling beige between the paisleys
Counting seasons on white knuckles
And now I sit ignoring this beat:
Floral upsweep on china receiving in clinks
Chipped mauve repetitions tapping
Identified – marked
By a bottle of nail varnish I know
From a bedside drawer
Proclaiming flower and time of day

I know my fingers strike
With the stern lustre of 'Twilight Rose' in tilted impatience
In a room melting to the back of a butter knife
With muffled small-talk and hyphened mercury rain
Keeping time with silver travelling to mouths
Your name is ill-contained here

An Unmaking

Come upon stairs curving a forest
Come upon a green sky low

Catch here your breath
Caught in vines in her hair
Her laugh caught in your bones and remember
The glass sound of children running down
Wrought metal steps open to night
They don't know the walls are gone replaced
Here and here by plaster dust
Rising to blush to freckles then nothing
Do not know here and here their voices fade
To plosives then nothing

Mind the beads on tiles broken
By bramble and wild heather
Mind the rust off the railings:

Its late leaves falling away
To gold to glitter then nothing

Mind this home unmade
Swallowed by a yawning moon
Unmoved by the fever of names
Wreathed in cape jasmine and the smallest clouds

Almost June

Now we make like wolves
And pull blue shadows across the snow
Approach this tree clump cut in plaster
Tonight this wall:
The damp makes it map
Her spare key, portal

Where mulled green stares in kitchen windows
And lampshade speaks this language full
Over hand starfished on my hip
And a pout where no name lived

We won't wear our words after sunrise
But if we step out now the moon
Will have us silver all the same
Our eyes clean and backs warm

Green

Full nest and forked tongue
Her heart spreads its hood
In the coiled thick of tree shade

Quick her venom
Twice pronged it burns sharp
Green shadows through the flesh

The colour of a closing day
The colour of one mother's rage
Wrapped in swathes of tender moss

Trees

Trees know how best to persist
And that, window's favourite one,
Makes me out to be
The still thing between us
Proclaiming season its thunderous life
A direction I cannot proceed
But only stumble through in part
Allergies, dry cleaning, soup

No surprise that it mocks
With its wild verdant announcements
Well, at least above the vulgar
Roots gnarling pavement pout,
And asphalt marred
All in wait for careless feet
As this canopy swallows my shadow
Down here:
Its shade a spread of many times
Its branches homes and open beaks

For summer
For the quiet so large
Yes, it is shade
And never shadow

And in one glance
The world becomes
Leaves

Craft

Burns her toes on palash flowers
Fallen in a fit of April

Her throat washed out with rain
She comes to draw the card
Chosen by a green bird
Until she knows him well

She braids her hair in promise
To Sutlej and her pale waters
Splitting homeland, cleaving hennaed palm
And now the hour blooms

She cuts through lemon at his doorstep
And watches it well with sour blood
The sure knowledge of nine lives more
Farther than vermillion, eyelash, bone

This is greater than a wedding day
This dripping of the candle wax
She adds a dark Kashmiri pepper
To the fire at the stove

And calls for storms to draw the night
From the other side of a mild moon
Shadows of a weeping sal
Eyes of a crow when she takes its shape
Watching him
Watching him

Shark

The bed adrift asks unsound thoughts
But this is no chance for books
Or pills

Somewhere a shark
Asleep mid-glide
Where kelp murks distance
Into brine magic lest it drown
A mortar-bound punch line
Thought up for the landlubbers who asked

Now don't go forgetting that
We and this
Make no kind of exchange.
Know most fish shy from conjecture
See it for a fan standing
Plugged-in poolside

And so we come to exhale
And skip the rows in
The wide pale mouths
Because: fair trade

Because: pride bitten bright
By unrequited awe reminds
Of far more promised back

Looks like tomorrow and after
Will keep their bits then
And we will become sleep
Silverware, dorsal fin, spacebar
And now your feet
Coming back to the safety of crisp sheets

Bucketsful

Soon someone will tell me
They remember the day
The frogs vanished

They were Dadi's lawn come alive
With rain in their bones
Asking about this and this and this
And just one in a bucket turned
The water a trembling green
Leaping to the rim
Like it knew a boiling hurry

One evening they left with summer
Never to return and only privately I think
It was because I forgot them
I forgot to watch the frogs of this city
And the water is bright no more

This I hold in my stomach
Where it prepares to climb
Pushing a sticky tongue to ask
If they all made it out

And if the far floodplains remain
Bits of mirror scattered on moss but of course
I won't say

Not until
The words balloon my throat and the only ones who would
    understand them
Have long skipped town

Crow

Picks herself out of bonemeal
Fading fingers, white of eye, she
Rises, unfurling
A thread of woodsmoke unspools
Throws back ash and lavender plume
And wails until

Long unheard
She curls now tight
Folding into shadow now
Tapering black scythe split to caw
Spreading wings cut from tonight
She searches her pyre

Burning done, smouldering done
She looks for her last name
Her favourite fruit
Her fullest year
Embers

Rubedo

It was in that vat the pieces burst
At first a sliver of candlelight
Held in a bubble stirring with
Froth and yoke and aqueous humour

And fibres stretched taut
Here into hair
Here into sinew
Straining under searing webs
Set to throb with pulse
As fingers shape, cooling
Over joints white-hot

And soon
She was bulbous head
Webbed fingers
A comma of spine
And peppercorn eyes

And soon
She will be over
And over again

Autopsy

We were just outside the shadows
Or inside, you could call it
A yellow island
Snowing dust

The naked bulb above the table
Flickered too much and I
Was more than a little afraid
That a moth might burn
And fall into you
As I traced the third incision
And pulled the pieces slowly open

And there, the clipped movie tickets
And there, a star calcified

Big Dark

The worst bit:
The streetlight halving shadows
On the ceiling, plaster, water-stained canvas

When night interrupts
And folds its legs on my chest
Slumping closer its eye
A plate of cold abalone
That murks too soon into slow green pictures
All in the clean breadth breathlessly parting

Chance from impending
Foothold from misstep
Bramble from wound

Until rest lowers to wading to plunging past
The froth of bed-linen florals where they dip to
Tar and the hardest thing to remember is
That night is the turn of a wild planet
For a time it makes the morning small

Before This Summer

Maybe this is how we ran afoul of spring
Pressed ourselves along the grass
And knew each blade with more than our toes
As we unhinged our ribs to devour the sun
All parts: hope and lemon and bird bones

Until full under a hunter's moon we waded
Past reed-fringed banks pushing
Ripples through the back of March
To tremble all the mirrors in our homes
Now parted in twos of world, roof and rice pot

It is how we came to break:
Things of a hard blue sky yearn
For the only light they do not share

For Patience

When asked to calm down again
Measure breath by the spoonful
Think molasses so that you remember an hour is thick
With seconds and glass and that if you breathe out all the way
Empty-chest-sharp all the way
The jagged bits will get you in the lungs

This is where names go to hide
Right up until the mouth
But only so far into the fire

Veils

Drift of double-ruled only
A hundred grams per square metre
And no fold pressed too close
So when it is done it shrugs bare to any
All that cools black or spice or blue
Strikethroughs notwithstanding

And it is done then, isn't it?
The name of the price evades
Like a gleaming small thing of
Adornment snatched from the
Site of ravishment to roll
Under your chair

Salome?
Draupadi?
Ishtar?
At all?

Crimson

I make no attempt to forget
That I could shed my religion to the smell of iron
Somewhere two-thousand-and-early
And am reminded in fact in every rush-hour knot
When raindrops pin taillights against the window
And let them trickle as it plays like
The alphabet; like I bit my lip
Bright like opening tinsel on his back in the throes
Like a spot you never see on a white skirt on TV
Though it remains truth, hers
The exile with thatch between her and that moon
Or the one with screens enough to confiscate
Kitchens and worship and all the world pressed small
Between fingers and thumbs of all the many

Too-little sons
Sculpting and chiselling and naming their gods new and
        ever old
While the truth in their veins has been down her thigh
More times than they know
More times than they know

Encroachment

Before we speak her hands lie flat
one over the other mooring the room
with the thread count of her kameez
not one crease left

in a stillness where summer cuts
loud and fat-yellow through the window
only to be staunched by
a raincloud at her cheek
dark with thunder
and one man's broken rage

until feet pound close outside
and all sound drains quick between:

squeaking hinges

creak of door

Sparrow

This is how we made our home:
Wove late winter into itself
And teased its tawny thatch into the cracks
So branches could swell to wagtail
And green-nosed petrichor

Sweeping more sky for a bloated spring
Bursting its gizzard to blow millet
Over the turf between your path and
The unmoored violence of thicket
Hiding dodder's wax bell

We settled in boughs for thorn
Never to spy yours closed within
The way you make your home
Folding asphalt over all the seasons
Moulting at your window

Blue

After their seas were no longer
Churning wine-dark

The mouth of a bruise
And corduroy belly of a whale

Spring draped flat over March
And the winking edge of glass

Came to lift a nursery far
Above all memory of the womb

Moth

They begin as dust
Powdering words that wait
For breath in quiet rooms

They stretch vowel to wing
That plosives oxidize to speckle
As inflection grows a downy
Brush of many legs

They spiral upwards in crescendo
Pitch rising to porch bulb
Filament orange-coiled and
Boiled in glass

Loud as another thing unsaid
Surely just enough to kindle
A new one for their tawny swarm
To live, to fly, to burn themselves

Crocodiles

She will winter here
When slate domes the city
And the sun opens small
A Jasper eye

She will watch from here
Trees unmade
The earth soaked
And the wheat sighing mist
Over the roads to let her once
Pretend she is not the only thing lost

When the light slants
And the river greens and pushes
Scales over its back
In a range of jagged peaks as sure
As teeth when it gapes in the sand
Now making ripples in her glass
Now waiting for her calloused feet

Slow Night

One of those evenings that stick

When your foot sinks so deep into the floor
You pull it out to find your kitten heel
Bearded with copper roots

Cloudbank stains window glass
Curtain cheesecloths grey from silver
And you cough up pomegranate seeds

Winking sharp as garnet

Pristine

This quiet is tidy
It has patience for boiled sweets
When much is to be spoken
It closes her lips
Sealing an envelope
Orchid cast on wax
Sheathing a love note
Destined for a shoebox under her bed

So clean this quiet
The world is the 3.00 a.m. street
And she the dust mote in the lamppost's beam
And he only passes through

Chenab Paar

The Chenab walks out of his waters
Mincing his steps as if on glass
Ready to be dressed by his pale groupies:
One with a rose, long past septic, in her chest
The other bluest at the lip and the third with silt
Burning through lungs where once the name
Mahiwal flowed an easy ebb

They kohl his eyes, brush his hair and again sing
Of the warmer springs that made
His banks loamy with verse
And then they move to new poetry
As if they move on glass

He is their patron god of romantic love
Lord of sweet nothings when in spate
Enough said: they have learnt to avoid good Faiz

A Stranger, Slowly

Fox fires on the canopy
Dim cold and slate
Raising horns and twitching ears
Sure as bone drumming firm from
Big cats waiting on wound or late calving
Listening now for snapping hot-season grass and –

Now the same is here
In the ink centre of tonight
Where just one word from
A stranger slowly downwind
Is enough to open the soles of her feet
Once woman in worn trainers
She is antelope again
Throat gulping for distance
Sprinting past green benches
Until the park gates she quakes the jogger's path
As it courses, pulses winding
Through hide and blue turf

Until finally the streetlights bloom wide enough
To blunt the jagged shadows and so it is all
Just a breeze in the bushes this once

The Undercity

The manhole buttons the tarmac firm
no secrets slip from a circle
until rain swells the way home
pooling grey around careless feet
when crooked hands now reach
now grasp

from the shivering undercity
upside-down and steely dun
and ripe as burnt rubber
where the eyes close to set firm
into discs rusted shut
and blue-collar throngs sail along
on 80s Bollywood posters
past the children strung with marigold
selling bombayduck and aliases and maps
to the way back up

Familiar Waters

By daylight the fires will be
Liver spots on the beach
And the sand gone from my hair

Still the girl will return
White-knuckled at the Arabian sea
So very sure a dorsal fin will rip it
From foam lip to bruised horizon
And so wide the slit will open
And so deep it will go with blue and green stars
She eclipses one by one
Picking her way first over
Sighing shells and then
The stonefish watching
Waves close white over her and I go
Home holding all I saw
The shark still swimming up and down my back

Mornings After

I watch her hungover
Her back going to frill
You know, the spinosaurus might have peacocked
For a go at gene immortality once
Not unlike this bent display
An emptying of her throat on a carpet she
Stares at so hard and new
Caught in the violence of woman versus colour

To be suddenly a thing with a stomach
On a span of plain pink:
Proud slant of light that is
Stained one instant, sunset the next
And remembered as young summer
Or opening love
And imagined as smear of afterbirth
Or a sky bright with meteors

Yes it hurts more than the sun
Sitting still to hold her fluid

She touches her face –
And it is still there, good
Good

Yellow

We live between forests
And cage small birds in our mouths
So when it comes time to go
Mining for what the old ones
Buried deep in the rock
Some of us might return

Holding Him

Sitting on the floor you think
It ought to taste like liquorice
The thick of the night
This night. Tonight, then?
Your place?

But for now it's best we pretend
You're not still pressing your foot
Down on a helpless soda can
Protesting in angry ting-pops
Because here you peel away

Talc smooth it overshadows
Routes from this place to another still
Making horizon in length
And line and row

I watch half-forgetting
It's not within whim to know him
It takes a cold thing and the city

For every alley down their throats
They have taught him
Crowbar and chain-link fence
Cardboard box, name in felt
And bottles you can tell
He has learnt through:

That theirs is the rain
But he is not quite so many

Maps

These borders are sunbaked

No – this is greyscale and
Stark of fissure in ex-ray

Bold line across a rib
Don't plaster them these days
Because of lungs, not that they'd never
Been there before the fall
Tributaries branched so plainly
All numbered homes and named streets

Marking in common
Directions in labyrinths of bone
Keeping cask, potion, sap, secret
Etched bus routes
They found winter hiding its paws in a box there

All of it committed, nevertheless
To paper in proof of her:
Cycles, history, allergies
As the screen blinks waiting

For ultrasound rumbling through
Palpating black and blue onto screen:
A star-sky seen through glass fogged by breath
She held so long looking
For Mars, Sothis, a heartbeat

Under fluorescent tubes
The kind that shadow hard
Square fingers running a pen
Over prescription or continent

Between Lipsticks and Forever

Try it on like any other lipstick but today
it's violet as description overripe,
it will look like I've bruised you
with a vengeance and alleged secret
so let me know, if I am selfish
when I say I don't care all we agree on are lotus stems
and maybe claw-footed bathtubs
though I could have always been
as wily as you pretend to believe

have me willing to believe when
I use the crook of your neck
for my share of privacy
when it comes to bartenders, old men,
the woman in the cab to our left,
maybe she'll lose pink somewhere
in your stubble thanks to
the taillights flooding in

while I paint on another smile
one not named for a summer confection
you think a shade too weak for me,

who has tasted more than wolves are allowed,

or so the crimson did suggest

when I last left it on your jawline though

there's no lamb here just a December night

That held its breath

to fit the tweed of a man

who one touch can make a place

that keeps out storm not fury,

except when it quiets so deep

I could still hear my voice

and the deference between

deadline and full stop,

subtitle and name,

all in the space you exhale

warm enough to thaw matte,

colour-intense guilt

as I try not to know

that I cannot repay you except

with that worn and hopeful threat:

his stars save him,

I mean to possess

The Descent

The woman fell out of the moon
With her fists closed on litchis and jasmine
Before she was a body
When she was a colour, a pixel
When she was a spot on the television news

And you knew at once to take the girl
By her hand saying no time, leave the crayons there
Call for your grandmother, bring the sheets and bottled water
The housemaid clatters over with plastic bags caught in
    her spine
Dropping her beads in the trail of fruit and laundry
And glass bangles and now you are at the door and
    now through
Feet padding old grass

The silver dust from a crater down the street
Would rush you any moment
A cloud to take the August sun
Announcing the woman who became the body
That became the spot
And now you brace for impact

Black

You, with nights under your fingernails
Tell no one how it happened

Say nothing of the shower stall
That spiral-drained you

Hair-first to fathoms below
Your chipped home

To a world so tepid green
The fireflies sail white

And higher still: familiar roads
Coil to stairwell yesteryears

Gone quiet now as ghost light
And you learn that even here

In fogged-mirror silence
Nothing

Is as still as you

Ant, Grasshopper

She found him
In a season the colour of apple cores
One man on the verge with
Gold hyphens slipping at his collarbones
And hunger enough to empty wicker baskets
Searching for girls with mouths of parijat

He meant small harm in smaller days
All for the price of a flight ticket
And days pressed to currants between
Pages folded for the edge of winter
And winters still

Origami

But said patience is for restless fingers
That have once, three times maybe, crisped a beak
Set the wings quick over my sister's ponytail
And tea smoke and finally
Mesh basket and after

It must remember
Palms that pressed a prow and
Party-hat triangle sail, and set it to bob
And right itself over wavelets opening pale
Left to grey to rain and curb

And now these fingertips
Close on newsprint and
Their papercuts purse tight
Fresh out of dailies and
Gloss lux and Chinese menu cards

And all it will take now is a final bend
Whitely down to impale yours truly

Cat

Or it may just be the light
Folded in glass
Exaggerations upon themselves
Orange onto flame,
Catching glints slipping pale, plain
In a plea too bright
Begging to be shattered
The slice of an inferno imagined

Whiskers ablaze
He is sated
And fish are real things

Beji

As it is told
I was three
And did not know that Beji had found her village
Brighter than ever
Behind her eyes

As it is told
I shouted the name for her
Straight at her sleeping face
Maybe squeezed her hand gnarled with roots
Ours

As I tell it
She found the place she knew
The breeze sharp as young limes
The wheat close and the colour of our skin
And where early mist is moon-smoke
Hiding Sahiban snapping arrows
Their sound spitting from kitchen fires

As I tell it
The old well she remembers
Is away from the homes of men
And in its bowels lie star-small bones

As Beji told it
She is alive and good enough

Tributary

It was end of schooldays
Mornings opened and feathers fell all the same
And there had been a crowd about the pyre

I was told, had to be told
Not having known the boy
A shape outside my orbits
My nineteen years of Plutos and feldspar
And talk of roots
Until his splintering close enough to see
How easily a tributary is made:
A young man slipping from the course of the day
His hours held close as cards

Ashes I think
Was the first word
Made of him becoming his bones
And then their grains turned full constellation
Reaching for skies he would never see
While staring brighter on new-moon nights

In other words, I remember his face
In other words, here is breakfast and meltwater

The Crossing Fields

Because habits survive death the new guys speak
Thait Punjabi and quarter moon
Down by the long wait where their peepul tree
Cracks the earth and borders between

This land and the far one
Soil and Sutlej water
Now and the sooty ever-after

They see none of those lines in chalk
And trace them green between easy bottles
That do the rounds about voting day or daybreak
Whichever comes quickest
Drawing flies that ask after the old man's hearing
State of harvest, the cows gone dry

Flour for a neighbour
And for a best friend chitta

White

And now we gather mogra
Fragrant in their grief

You know we wear white in yearning
Reading from pyre smoke

In this way, we are brittle femur
And like this, we are sky

Acknowledgements

This book exists because of luck, introspection, and many, many people.

I am grateful to HarperCollins Publishers India.

To Udayan Mitra, for his faith in these poems.

To writer, editor and friend, Sohini Basak, with whom conversation has a way of letting the seasons in, even through office windows.

To Shantanu Ray Chaudhuri, for all the encouragement.

To Hartosh Bal, for an introduction to the world of publishing.

To the Sahitya Akademi journal, *Indian Literature* for featuring my poems 'The Dollmaker', 'Seven', 'Origami', 'Lipstick and Forever', 'Rain', 'Postscript', 'Neighbour', 'The Artist's Demonstration' and 'Green' in the May-June 2018 issue.

To Sampurna Chattarji and *The Indian Quarterly*, for first publishing 'Or Not Drowning', 'Cat', 'Gloria', 'Indiscretion', 'Pristine' and 'Beji' (Volume 7; issue 2; January–March 2019).

To Dharmendra Deol, Arundhathi Subramaniam, Chitra Banerjee Divakaruni, Tabish Khair, Shabana Azmi and Twinkle Khanna for their kind words about this book.

And to those who make up my life:

Thank you, Mom and Dad for everything I am.

Thank you, Sahil, for strength.

Thank you, Pulkit, for love.

Thank you, Anahat, for being.

About the Author

Prerna Gill is a writer and editor. Her poems have appeared in *Indian Literature*, the Sahitya Akademi bimonthly journal, and in *The Indian Quarterly*. Her work has also appeared in the anthology *A Poem a Day* by Gulzar, published by HarperCollins Publishers India.

30 Years *of*

HarperCollins *Publishers* India

At HarperCollins, we believe in telling the best stories and finding the widest possible readership for our books in every format possible. We started publishing 30 years ago; a great deal has changed since then, but what has remained constant is the passion with which our authors write their books, the love with which readers receive them, and the sheer joy and excitement that we as publishers feel in being a part of the publishing process.

Over the years, we've had the pleasure of publishing some of the finest writing from the subcontinent and around the world, and some of the biggest bestsellers in India's publishing history. Our books and authors have won a phenomenal range of awards, and we ourselves have been named Publisher of the Year the greatest number of times. But nothing has meant more to us than the fact that millions of people have read the books we published, and somewhere, a book of ours might have made a difference.

As we step into our fourth decade, we go back to that one word – a word which has been a driving force for us all these years.

Read.